500 Things

Your Minister Tried To Tell You

500 Things

Your Minister Tried To Tell You

...But the guy sitting next to you was snoring so loud you couldn't hear.

Written and Compiled by
JEANIE PRICE

Star Song Publishing Group
a division of Jubilee Communications, Inc.
P.O. Box 150009
Nashville, Tennessee 37215

ISBN # 1-56233-087-X

Printed in the United States of America
First Printing, September 1993

1 2 3 4 5 6 7 8 9 – 97 96 95 94 93

If everyone with whom I shared the Gospel
gave their heart to Christ except for even one member of my family
then I would consider my life to be an abject failure.

—JAMES L. MATHEWS

Life, if properly viewed in any aspect, is great, but mainly great
when viewed in its relation to the world to come.

—ALBERT BARNES

The steady discipline of intimate friendship with Jesus
results in men becoming like Him.

—HARRY EMERSON FOSDICK

Let your conversation be always
full of grace, seasoned with salt, so that you may know how to
answer everyone. *Colossians 4:6*

—ST. PAUL

To saints their very slumber is a prayer.

—ST. JEROME

Better to fail here (as fail we must) than not to try; for failure
may bring us to a deeper understanding.

—GEORGE A. BUTTRICK

If we were to be asked suddenly to give a definition of humility,
we would doubtless be greatly embarrassed.

—EDWIN HOLT HUGHES

For with much wisdom comes much sorrow;
the more knowledge, the more grief. *Ecclesiastes 1:18*

—SOLOMON, "THE PREACHER"

The noblest charities, the best fruits of learning,
the richest discoveries, the best institutions of law and justice,
every greatest thing the world has seen, represents, more
or less directly, the fruitfulness and creativeness of religion.

—HORACE BUSHNELL

An undivided heart which worships God alone,
and trusts him as it should, is raised above anxiety for earthly wants.

—CUNNINGHAM GEIKIE

For I am convinced that neither death nor life, neither angels nor demons, neither the present nor the future, nor any powers, neither height nor depth, nor anything else in all creation, will be able to seperate us from the love of God that is in Christ Jesus our Lord. *Romans 8:38-39*

—ST. PAUL

The brotherhood of man is an integral part of Christianity no less than the Fatherhood of God; and to deny the one is no less infidel than to deny the other.

—LYMAN ABBOTT

Whoever loves money never has money enough; whoever loves wealth is never satisfied with his income. This too is meaningless. *Ecclesiastes 5:10*

—SOLOMON, "THE PREACHER"

The flower of youth never appears more beautiful than when it bends toward the sun of righteousness.

—MATTHEW HENRY

In his life, Christ is an example, showing us how to live; in his death, he is a sacrifice, satisfying for our sins; in his resurrection, a conqueror; in his ascension, a king; in his intercession, a high priest.

—MARTIN LUTHER

Behold, I will create new heavens and a new earth. The former things will not be remembered, nor will they come to mind. *Isaiah 65:17*

—ISAIAH, THE PROPHET

Religion is the fear and love of God; its demonstration is good works; and faith is the root of both, for without faith we cannot please God; nor can we fear and love what we do not believe.

—WILLIAM PENN

Devote yourselves to prayer,
being watchful and thankful. *Colossians 4:2*

—ST. PAUL

No man is to be crowned simply because he is gifted. Large gifts do not reflect credit upon the receiver, but upon the Giver.

—CLOVIS G. CHAPPELL

Men ask for excitement, when they need enthusiasm.
They ask for solace, when they need salvation.
They seek the sensual, when they need the spiritual. Everywhere
men are asking for goods, when they need God.
Yet the cry comes out of a need that is profound. The trouble is
that men do not understand their own need.

—G. CAMPBELL MORGAN

Don't have anything to do with foolish and stupid arguments,
because you know they produce quarrels. *2 Timothy 2:23*

—ST. PAUL

One's life is his capital, not his circumstances.

—JAMES I. VANCE

Therefore, I urge you, brothers, in view of God's mercy,
to offer your bodies as living sacrifices, holy and pleasing to God—
this is your spiritual act of worship. *Romans 12:1*

—ST. PAUL

How fast we learn in a day of sorrow!
Scripture shines out in a new effulgence; every verse seems
to contain a sunbeam, every promise
stands out in illuminated splendor; things hard to be
understood become in a moment plain.

—HORATIUS BONAR

For God will bring every deed into judgment, including
every hidden thing, whether it is good or evil. *Ecclesiastes 12:14*

—SOLOMON, "THE PREACHER"

Information alone will not change your life.
Revelation in your spirit is what produces change. In fact, that is
how a friend of mine differentiates between information
and revelation. He says, "When you have revelation in your spirit,
there will be immediate change."

—DON CROSSLAND

Anyone who does wrong will be repaid for his wrong,
and there is no favoritism. *Colossians 3:25*

—ST. PAUL

All human legislation should accord with
the divine code, but does not. Hence many things are legal that
are not morally right.

—W.T. USSERY

Better limp all the way to heaven than not get there at all.

—WILLIAM A. ("BILLY") SUNDAY

Avoid godless chatter, because those who indulge in it will become more and more ungodly. *2 Timothy 2:16*

—ST. PAUL

A Christian graveyard is a cradle, where, in the quiet motions of the globe, Jesus rocks his sleeping children. By and by he will wake them from their slumber, and in the arms of angels they shall be translated to the skies.

—GEORGE B. CHEEVER

The body of our prayer is the sum of our duty;
and as we must ask of God whatsoever we need, so we must
watch and labor for all that we ask.

—JEREMY TAYLOR

Do not be quick with your mouth, do not be hasty in
your heart to utter anything before God. God is in heaven and you
are on earth, so let your words be few. *Ecclesiastes 5:2*

—SOLOMON, "THE PREACHER"

So when our minds are so distracted and our thoughts
become muddied and muddled, we can look up to
the Christ and rise into a high mindedness where little things
and petty puzzlements do not reach us.

—RALPH W. SOCKMAN

Do not conform any longer to the pattern of this world,
but be transformed by the renewing of your mind.
Then you will be able to test and approve what God's will is—
his good, pleasing and perfect will. *Romans 12:2*

—ST. PAUL

Science and religion no more
contradict each other than light and electricity.

—WILLIAM HIRAM FOULKES

Do your best to present yourself to God as
one approved, a workman who does not need to be ashamed and
who correctly handles the word of truth. *2 Timothy 2:15*

—ST. PAUL

God sometimes washes the eyes of his children with tears that they may read aright his providence and his commandments.

—THEODORE L. CUYLER

In self-examination, take no account of yourself by your thoughts and resolutions in the days of religion and solemnity, but examine how it is with you in the days of ordinary conversation and in the circumstances of secular employment.

—JEREMY TAYLOR

Hear this, you foolish and senseless people, who have eyes but do not see, who have ears but do not hear: "Should you not fear me?" declares the LORD. "Should you not tremble in my presence? I made the sand a boundary for the sea, an everlasting barrier it cannot cross. The waves may roll, but they cannot prevail; they may roar, but they cannot cross it." *Jeremiah 5:21-22*

—JEREMIAH, THE PROPHET

If the prayer of one or two has great avail, how much more that of the total Church.

—IGNATIUS OF ANTIOCH

And the Lord's servant must not quarrel; instead, he must be kind to everyone, able to teach, not resentful. *2 Timothy 2:24*

—ST. PAUL

The hope of the world is in the hands of those who will not take counsel of despair.

—JOSEPH R. SIZOO

Lovely flowers are the smiles of God's goodness.

—WILLIAM WILBERFORCE

Command those who are rich in this present world not to be arrogant nor to put their hope in wealth, which is so uncertain, but to put their hope in God, who richly provides us with everything for our enjoyment. *1 Timothy 6:17*

—ST. PAUL

Anxiety is a word of unbelief or unreasoning dread. We have no right to allow it. Full faith in God puts it to rest.

—HORACE BUSHNELL

We are immortal until our work on earth is done.

—GEORGE WHITEFIELD

As you do not know the path of the wind, or how
the body is formed in a mother's womb, so you cannot understand
the work of God, the Maker of all things. *Ecclesiastes 11:5*

—SOLOMON, "THE PREACHER"

The study of God's Word,
for the purpose of discovering God's will, is the secret discipline
which has formed the greatest characters.

—JAMES W. ALEXANDER

Whatever you do, work at it with all your heart,
as working for the Lord, not for men, since you know that you will
receive an inheritance from the Lord as a reward.
It is the Lord Christ you are serving. *Colossians 3:23-24*

—ST. PAUL

Do you ever sit down and wonder what is wrong with
the world? Do you ever ask yourself why it is that Christians seem
to have so little influence, why they seem to achieve
so little, for all their numbers, in putting the world right?
To each of those two questions there is ultimately but one answer.
It is this: we lack the mind of Christ.

—J. ARTHUR LEWIS

And whatever you do, whether in word or deed,
do it all in the name of the Lord Jesus, giving thanks to God the
Father through him. *Colossians 3:17*

—ST. PAUL

If you don't want to take your character from your environment
but to put character into it, you will need to
draw on spiritual resources greater than your own. And you may.
You can be strengthened by God in your inner life if
you will open it daily to His influence. It was of this Paul was
thinking when he said: "Be not conformed to
this world but be ye transformed by the renewing of your mind."

—ROBERT JAMES MCCRACKEN

For the love of money is a root of all kinds of evil.
Some people, eager for money, have wandered from the faith and
pierced themselves with many griefs. *1 Timothy 6:10*

—ST. PAUL

To love is not a passive thing. "To love" is active voice.
When I love I do something, I function, I give. I do not love in order
that I may be loved back again, but for the
creative joy of loving. And every time I do so love I am freed,
at least a little, by the outgoing of love, from
enslavement to that most intolerable of master, myself.

—BERNARD IDDINGS BELL

All that I am I owe
to Jesus Christ, revealed to me in His Divine Book.

—DAVID LIVINGSTONE

Better a poor but wise youth than an old but foolish king who no longer knows how to take warning. *Ecclesiastes 4:13*

—SOLOMON, "THE PREACHER"

Anyone who is to find Christ must first find the church.
How could anyone know where Christ is
and what faith in him is unless he knew where his believers are?

—MARTIN LUTHER

Love must be sincere.
Hate what is evil; cling to what is good. *Romans 12:9*

—ST. PAUL

What is the chief end of man? You know the answer.
The chief end of man is to glorify God and to enjoy Him forever.
Christ gives us peace with joy.
It is the purpose of God in Christ that the deepest desires of the
human heart should be forever satisfied.

—RUSSELL CARTWRIGHT STROUP

The greatest part of life is
adjusting ourselves to circumstances. It is only in daydreams
that we are able to control our fate.

—WALTER DALE LANGTRY

People who want to get rich fall into temptation and
a trap and into many foolish and harmful desires that plunge men
into ruin and destruction. *1 Timothy 6:9*

—ST. PAUL

Let us then, brothers, be humble and be rid
of all pretensions and arrogance and silliness and anger.
Let us act as Scripture bids us.

—CLEMENT OF ROME

Bear with each other and
forgive whatever grievances you may have against one another.
Forgive as the Lord forgave you. *Colossians 3:13*

—ST. PAUL

When I was young, I was sure of many things; now there are
only two things of which I am sure: one is, that I am
a miserable sinner; and the other, that Christ is an all-sufficient
Saviour. He is well-taught who learns these two lessons.

—JOHN NEWTON

For we brought nothing into the world,
and we can take nothing out of it. *1 Timothy 6:7*

—ST. PAUL

It is only Christianity, the great bond of love and duty to God,
that makes any existence valuable or even tolerable.

—HORACE BUSHNELL

I was baptized with the Holy Spirit
when I took Him by simple faith in the Word of God.

—R.A. TORREY

Therefore, as God's chosen people, holy and dearly loved,
clothe yourselves with compassion, kindness,
humility, gentleness and patience. *Colossians 3:12*

—ST. PAUL

A loving trust in the Author of the Bible is the best preparation for a wise and profitable study of the Bible itself.

—HENRY CLAY TRUMBELL

S ow your seed in the morning, and at evening let not your hands be idle, for you do not know which will succeed, whether this or that, or whether both will do equally well. *Ecclesiastes 11:6*

—SOLOMON, "THE PREACHER"

I f every church in our land today could boast that in its gatherings Christ is king and its people ready, having heard the voice of Christ, to go to work democratically to do his will, what a Church, what a land, we should have!

—DOUGLAS HORTON

Nobody ever outgrows Scripture;
the book widens and deepens with our years.

—CHARLES SPURGEON

This is what the LORD says: "Let not the wise man boast of
his wisdom or the strong man boast of his strength or the rich man
boast of his riches, but let him who boasts boast about this:
that he understands and knows me, that I am the LORD,
who exercises kindness, justice and righteousness on earth, for in
these I delight," declares the LORD. *Jeremiah 9:23-24*

—JEREMIAH, THE PROPHET

The minority with a mission must bow again before the Master,
and moving out with a message incarnate, certain life
everlasting, take up the Cross anew, risk all, and thus save all.

—JOHN F. CRONIN

Be devoted to one another in brotherly love.
Honor one another above yourselves. *Romans 12:10*
—ST. PAUL

Carnal people cannot act spiritually, or spiritual people carnally,
just as faith cannot act like unbelief, or unbelief like faith.
But even what you do in the flesh you do spiritually. For you do
everything under Christ's control.
—IGNATIUS OF ANTIOCH

To holy people the very name of Jesus is
a name to feed upon, a name to transport. His name can raise
the dead and transfigure and beautify the living.
—JOHN HENRY NEWMAN

Two are better than one, because they have a good
return for their work: If one falls down, his friend can help him up.
But pity the man who falls and has no one to help him up!

Ecclesiastes 4:9-10

—SOLOMON, "THE PREACHER"

No one can save all men,
but each of us can save some men.

—HARRY V. RICHARDSON

Do not lie to each other, since you have taken off your
old self with its practices and have put on
the new self, which is being renewed in knowledge in the
image of its Creator. *Colossians 3:9-10*

—ST. PAUL

The joy of unselfish love is the purest joy that man can taste;
the joy of perfect self-sacrifice is the highest joy
that humanity can possess; and they lie open for us all.

—ALEXANDER MACLAREN

But godliness with contentment is
great gain. *1 Timothy 6:6*

—ST. PAUL

God wills that all men might be saved.
But it is necessary that they cooperate in this, that they consent
to this, that they do not refuse his Grace, which calls them.

—MICHEL RIQUET

Temptation conquered is
Christian character strengthened.
—BERTHA MUNRO

Never be lacking in zeal, but keep your spiritual fervor,
serving the Lord. *Romans 12:11*
—ST. PAUL

If a man cannot be a Christian in the place he is,
he cannot be a Christian anywhere.
—HENRY WARD BEECHER

If a man is lazy, the rafters sag;
if his hands are idle, the house leaks. *Ecclesiastes 10:18*
—SOLOMON, "THE PREACHER"

We have seen that the cross was necessary to break the power of sin and that it was inescapable even for the Son of God. But we must not fail to apprehend its personal implications for ourselves. To believe on Christ, to accept him as one's personal Savior and Lord, is to die to self and live for God regardless of the consequences.

—WALTER N. ROBERTS

Men are more accountable for their motives, than for anything else; and primarily, morality consists in the motives, that is in the affections.

—ARCHIBALD ALEXANDER

The elders who direct the affairs of the church well are worthy of double honor, especially those whose work is preaching and teaching. *1 Timothy 5:17*

—ST. PAUL

Sufficient to each day are the duites to be done and the trials to be endured. God never built a Christian strong enough to carry today's duties and tomorrow's anxieties piled on the top of them.

—THEODORE L. CUYLER

But now you must rid yourselves of all such things as these: anger, rage, malice, slander, and filthy language from your lips. *Colossians 3:8*

—ST. PAUL

For health and the constant enjoyment of life,
give me a keen and ever-present sense of humor; it is the next best
thing to an abiding faith in providence.

—GEORGE B. CHEEVER

Wanted: Christian Gamblers who will not sit by the campfire
but will push out into the social underbrush where
it is dangerous to go and where a man has to risk his life.
Wanted: Christian Gamblers who will scorn taking
cheap chances for the flashy impermanent rewards of the world
and will bet their lives on God and His purposes.
Wanted: Christians who will gamble that Jesus is right and
has a claim to their complete allegiance.

—GERALD KENNEDY

Whatever is has already been,
and what will be has been before; and God will call the past
to account. *Ecclesiastes 3:15*

—SOLOMON, "THE PREACHER"

A defiled spirit can be cleansed; a dulled sensitivity to God
can be sharpened. The cleansing comes when we
confess our sin to God. We must confess the lies about God we
believed and the sinful acts, the mistrust, and separation
from God which those beliefs resulted in. After we ask God to
forgive us, we must repent and change our ways.

—DON CROSSLAND

Be joyful in hope,
patient in affliction, faithful in prayer. *Romans 12:12*

—ST. PAUL

We are certain that there is forgiveness,
because there is a Gospel, and the very essence of the Gospel lies
in the proclamation of the pardon of sin.

—CHARLES HADDON SPURGEON

If you keep your feet from breaking the Sabbath and
from doing as you please on my holy day, if you call the Sabbath
a delight and the LORD's holy day honorable, and if you
honor it by not going your own way and not doing as you please or
speaking idle words, then you will find your joy in the LORD,
and I will cause you to ride on the heights of the land and to feast
on the inheritance of your father Jacob. *Isaiah 58:13-14*

—ISAIAH, THE PROPHET

God never permits an evil without good coming from it.

—FULTON J. SHEEN

Set your minds on things above, not on earthly things.

Colossians 3:2

—ST. PAUL

Today we live, move, and have our being in the abdomen of God.
We live and move and have our being in God
even though we cannot see the face of God. Now the baby,
having made these observations, may think,
"Oh, I am indeed a great philosopher." But we know that baby is
very presumptuous. So with us.
As long as we remain materialistically minded, we are like
that baby—very presumptuous.

—TOYOHIKO KAGAWA

The fullest Christian experience is simply the fullest life.

—PHILLIPS BROOKS

Watch your life and doctrine closely.
Persevere in them, because if you do, you will save both yourself
and your hearers. *1 Timothy 4:16*

—ST. PAUL

Only out of struggle and pain can there come the kind
of person and the kind of world that
the wisdom and power and goodness of God are set to make.
How could you teach any man courage if
there were no fears to fight, no threats to overcome?

—HERBERT WELCH

Essential Christianity must be original Christianity, Christianity as the Founder presented it, before the distorting, disintegrating influences of history had borne down upon it, before it had attracted to itself alien interests, and contracted compromising affinities, Christianity in the simplicity of its beginnings, in the unspotted purity of its new birth—in a word, the Christianity, and not the Christianity of Christendom.

—HERBERT HENSLEY HENSON

To the man who pleases him, God gives wisdom, knowledge and happiness, but to the sinner he gives the task of gathering and storing up wealth to hand it over to the one who pleases God. This too is meaningless, a chasing after the wind. *Ecclesiastes 2:26*

—SOLOMON, "THE PREACHER"

The Christian needs a reminder every hour; some defeat, surprise, adversity, peril; to be agitated, mortified, beaten out of his course, so that all remains of self will be sifted out.

—HORACE BUSHNELL

It's not the rules and regulations you follow carefully that will win you favor with God but rather offering your life to Him in complete faith that His Son, Jesus Christ, conquered sin and death on your behalf and for your salvation.

—JAMES L. MATHEWS

Do not let anyone who delights in false humility and the worship of angels disqualify you for the prize. Such a person goes into great detail about what he has seen, and his unspiritual mind puffs him up with idle notions. *Colossians 2:18*

—ST. PAUL

God has made of one blood all who
dwell upon the face of the earth. They are our brothers and sisters.
Let us learn to treat them so. Many of the children
of earth have not the Gospel. Let us hurry to take or send good
news of Christ's love to them all.

—G.B.F. HALLOCK

God is like the sun at high noon, always giving all he has.

—ARTHUR JOHN GOSSIP

This is what the LORD says:
"Maintain justice and do what is right, for my salvation
is close at hand and my
righteousness will soon be revealed." *Isaiah 56:1*

—ISAIAH, THE PROPHET

'Tis not for man to trifle; life is brief, and sin is here.
We have no time to sport away the hours; all must be earnest in
a world like ours.

—HORATIUS BONAR

Share with God's people who are in need.
Practice hospitality. *Romans 12:13*

—ST. PAUL

As the print of the seal on the wax is the express image
of the seal itself, so Christ is
the express image—the perfect representation of God.

—AMBROSE OF MILAN

For everything God created is good, and nothing is to be rejected if it is received with thanksgiving, because it is consecrated by the word of God and prayer. *1 Timothy 4:4-5*

—ST. PAUL

There cannot be named a pursuit or enterprise of human beings, in which there is so little possibility of failure, as praying for sanctification.

—JAMES W. ALEXANDER

The greatest negative in the universe is the Cross, for with it God wiped out everything that was not of himself; the greatest positive in the universe is the resurrection, for through it God brought into being all he will have in the new creation.

—WATCHMAN NEE

49

See to it that no one takes you captive through hollow and deceptive philosophy, which depends on human tradition and the basic principles of this world rather than on Christ. *Colossians 2:8*

—ST. PAUL

It would be a blessed thing for our society if we could contemplate sin from the same point of view from which Christ and his apostles saw it.

—FREDERICK WILLIAM ROBERTSON

There is a time for everything, and a season for every activity under heaven. *Ecclesiastes 3:1*

—SOLOMON, "THE PREACHER"

Try to gather together more frequently to celebrate God's
Eucharist and to praise him. For when you meet with frequency,
Satan's powers are overthrown and his
destructiveness is undone by the unanimity of your faith.

—IGNATIUS OF ANTIOCH

When you are tempted to do wrong ask
the Saviour to help you. Seek His grace, His strength, His blessing
in everything you do. Let His love control all your thoughts and
actions. America needs more boys and girls, more men and women
whose hearts are great, whose purposes are pure, and
whose lives are fragrant with kindness, truthfulness, and honesty.

—ALFRED BARRATT

And my God will meet all your needs
according to his glorious riches in Christ Jesus. *Philippians 4:19*

—ST. PAUL

Respectable sin is, in principle, the mother of
all basest crime. Follow it to the bitter end, and there is ignominy
as well as guilt eternal.

—HORACE BUSHNELL

For since the creation of the world God's invisible qualities—
his eternal power and divine nature—
have been clearly seen, being understood from what has been
made, so that men are without excuse. *Romans 1:20*

—ST. PAUL

In front of you lies your life. There will be many hard things to do, many a cross to carry. Christ says to you, "Take up every difficult task, every unpleasant duty, every cross; take them up one by one." You will often think that you cannot bear them. Try! Trying develops wings. The cross will turn into strong pinions that will carry you over every trouble and sorrow, over every difficulty; and by and by these same pinions will enable you to overvault the dark valley of death, and then you will awake in His likeness. Take up every duty. Trust in God. The weights will become wings and bear you heavenward.

—JAMES LEARMOUNT

When God wants to speak and deal with us, he does not avail himself of an angel but of parents, or the pastor, or of our neighbor.

—MARTIN LUTHER

I know that everything God does will endure forever;
nothing can be added to it and
nothing taken from it. God does it, so men will revere him.

Ecclesiastes 3:14

—SOLOMON, "THE PREACHER"

Paying of debts is, next to the grace of God,
the best means of delivering you from a thousand temptations
to vanity and sin.

—PATRICK DELANY

Bless those who persecute you; bless and
do not curse. *Romans 12:14*

—ST. PAUL

There is one case of death-bed repentance recorded, that of the penitent thief, that none should despair; and only one that none should presume.

—ST. AUGUSTINE

Whatever is true, whatever is noble, whatever is right, whatever is pure, whatever is lovely, whatever is admirable—if anything is excellent or praiseworthy— think about such things. *Philippians 4:8*

—ST. PAUL

Of all commentaries upon the Scriptures, good examples are the best and the livliest.

—JOHN DONNE

$\mathbb{F}$or it is not those who hear the law who
are righteous in God's sight, but it is those who obey the law who
will be declared righteous. *Romans 2:13*

—ST. PAUL

$\mathbb{W}$hat matters, is not what we appear to be on the outside, but
what we have in us to become. We may seem to be very
insignificant and unattractive outwardly, but if we have the love of
Jesus in our hearts, then, although we may say, "It doth
not yet appear what we shall be," we can go on to say, as John did,
"But we know that some day we shall be like him."

—J.C. COMPTON

It is right, then, and holy, brothers, that we should obey God rather than follow those arrogant and disorderly fellows who take the lead in stirring up loathsome rivalry. For we shall incur no ordinary harm, but rather great danger, if we recklessly give ourselves over to the designs of men who launch into strife and sedition to alienate us from what is right.

—CLEMENT OF ROME

A man can do nothing better than to eat and drink and find satisfaction in his work. This too, I see, is from the hand of God, for without him, who can eat or find enjoyment? *Ecclesiastes 2:24-25*

—SOLOMON, "THE PREACHER"

Stimulate the heart to love, and all other virtues will rise of their own accord.

—W.T. USSERY

Do not be anxious about anything, but in everything, by prayer and petition, with thanksgiving, present your requests to God.

Philippians 4:6

—ST. PAUL

Men are doubtful and skeptical about the Church; they suspect and dislike the clergy: they are impatient of theological systems; but for Jesus Christ, as he stand out to view in the sacred pages, as they dimly realize him in their own best selves, as they catch faint traces of him in the lives of his saints, they have no other sentiments than those of respect and affection.

—HERBERT HENSLEY HENSON

The more man becomes irradiated with
the Divinity of Christ, the more, not the less, truly he is man.

—PHILLIPS BROOKS

Rejoice with those who rejoice;
mourn with those who mourn. *Romans 12:15*

—ST. PAUL

Our opportunities to do good are our talents.

—COTTON MATHER

I know, O Lord, that a man's life is
not his own; it is not for man to direct his steps. *Jeremiah 10:23*

—JEREMIAH, THE PROPHET

If God remembers the creeping and crawling things that obey His
laws and calls them to another world after they have finished
their life in the pool, surely He will remember His children who
love and serve Him and call them to a world more beautiful
and wonderful than this when they finish their life here on earth.

—R. ALBERT GOODWIN

I never knew a child of God being bankrupted
by his benevolence. What we keep we may lose, but what we give
to Christ we are sure to keep.

—THEODORE L. CUYLER

Let no debt remain outstanding, except the continuing debt
to love one another, for he who loves
his fellowman has fulfilled the law. *Romans 13:8*

—ST. PAUL

Faith in tomorrow,
instead of Christ, is Satan's nurse for man's perdition.

—GEORGE B. CHEEVER

It does not require great learning to be a Christian and be
convinced of the truth of the Bible. It requires only an honest heart
and a willingness to obey God.

—ALBERT BARNES

Much dreaming and many words are meaningless.
Therefore stand in awe of God. *Ecclesiastes 5:7*

—SOLOMON, "THE PREACHER"

You need not worry about where you yourself are.
You watch your thoughts or ideals.
If your thoughts or ideals are in the right, it will not be long before
you yourself will be there, but, on the other hand,
if your thoughts or ideals are bad, it will not be long before you
will be there. If you want to be sure of
your thoughts and your ideals all you need to do is to center
them upon Jesus Christ and what He would
have you do, and everything will be right with you.

—LESLIE E. DUNKIN

Let your gentleness be evident to all. The Lord is near.

Philippians 4:5

—ST. PAUL

Just think what a different world this old earth soon might become if we imitated the flowers and took as much pleasure in comforting the poor as in catering to the whims of the rich. And if we would live without pride and give of our worldly possessions to satisfy the needs of humanity; if we would obey the second great commandment given by our Lord, "Thou shalt love thy neighbor as thyself" *Matthew 5:43*, then we, like flowers, could live without anxiety and die without pain.

—ROBERT LEE CAMPBELL

To know whom you worship, let me see you in your shop, let me overhear you in your trade; let me know how you rent your houses, how you get your money, how you keep it, or how it is spent.

—THEODORE PARKER

The LORD said, "Surely I will deliver you for a good purpose;
surely I will make your enemies plead with
you in times of disaster and times of distress." *Jeremiah 15:11*
—JEREMIAH, THE PROPHET

It is as natural and reasonable for a dependent creature to apply
to its Creator for what it needs, as for a child to solicite
the aid of a parent who is believed to have the disposition and
ability to bestow what it needs.
—ARCHIBALD ALEXANDER

Live in harmony with one another.
Do not be proud, but be willing to associate with people of
low position. Do not be conceited. *Romans 12:16*
—ST. PAUL

The Holy Spirit makes a man a Christian, and if he is
a Christian through the work of the Holy Spirit,
that same Spirit draws him to other Christians in the church.
An individual Christian is no Christian at all.

—R. BROKHOFF

All light that does not proceed from God is false; it only dazzles
us; it sheds no illumination upon the difficult paths in which we
must walk, along the precipices that are about us.

—FRANCOIS FENELON

Rather, clothe yourselves with
the Lord Jesus Christ, and do not think about how to gratify the
desires of the sinful nature. *Romans 13:14*

—ST. PAUL

It would be a good thing if every one of us made
a vow that we would never pass on a criticism of another person
without having first made an honest try to
clear it up with the person immediately involved.

—SAMUEL M. SHOEMAKER

We have been taught the art of being strenuous,
and we have lost the art of being still.

—GEORGE H. MORRISON

Remember your Creator in the days of your youth,
before the days of trouble come and the years approach when you
will say, "I find no pleasure in them." *Ecclesiastes 12:1*

—SOLOMON, "THE PREACHER"

The church of Jesus Christ belongs to no class or race.
—DUKE M. MCCALL

Rejoice in the Lord always.
I will say it again: Rejoice! *Philippians 4:4*
—ST. PAUL

Of all the duties enjoined by Christianity, none is more essential and yet more neglected, than prayer.
—FRANCOIS DE SALIGNAC DE LA MOTHE FENELON

How sweet the name of Jesus sounds in a believer's ears!
—JOHN NEWTON

My religion is not vital until my heart is in it.
Christ is not a real power in my life until he gets into my heart,
for the heart is the seat of the affections.

—RALPH W. SOCKMAN

Accept him whose faith is weak, without passing judgment on
disputable matters. *Romans 14:1*

—ST. PAUL

Now the church is not wood and stone,
but the company of people who believe in Christ.

—MARTIN LUTHER

But our citizenship is in heaven. And we eagerly await a Savior
from there, the Lord Jesus Christ. *Philippians 3:20*

—ST. PAUL

Children as soon as they can understand ought to be told about Jesus Christ, that they may make him the hero of their young lives.

—GERARD MANLEY HOPKINS

Though one may be overpowered, two can defend themselves. A cord of three strands is not quickly broken. *Ecclesiastes 4:12*

—SOLOMON, "THE PREACHER"

You may deface the image of God, but you can never erase it.

—JOSEPH R. SIZOO

The living Christ is not a possession to be bought, or a commodity to exchanged. To know him we must give ourselves to him.

—WALTER DALE LANGTRY

Do not repay anyone evil for evil.
Be careful to do what is right in the eyes of everybody.

Romans 12:17

—ST. PAUL

It is possible to love your friends, your competitors,
and even your enemies. It is hard, bitterly hard, but there is a long
distance between hard and impossible.

—HERBERT WELCH

"For my thoughts are not your thoughts,
neither are your ways my ways," declares the Lord. *Isaiah 55:8*

—ISAIAH, THE PROPHET

A man of a right spirit is not a man of narrow and private
views, but is greatly interested and concerned for
the good of the community to which he belongs, and particularly
of the city or village in which he resides,
and for the true welfare of the society of which he is a member.

—JONATHAN EDWARDS

Lay hold of the pathway which leads towards heaven; rugged
and narrow as it is, lay hold of it, and journey on.
And how will you be able to do these things? By subduing the
body, and bringing it into subjection.
For when the way grows narrow, the obesity that comes of
gluttony is a great hindrance.

—JOHN CHRYSOSTOM

Accept one another, then,
just as Christ accepted you, in order to bring praise to God.

Romans 15:7

—ST. PAUL

Shun evil of every kind. For how shall he who cannot govern
himself in these things teach another?

—POLYCARP OF SMYRNA

Only let us live up to what we have already attained.

Philippians 3:16

—ST. PAUL

The wind changes the atmosphere,
the fire changes the temperature; but when you have changed
the atmosphere and temperature of
a soul you have accomplished a mighty transformation.

—JOHN HENRY JOWETT

Be happy, young man, while you are young, and let
your heart give you joy in the days of your youth.
Follow the ways of your heart and whatever your eyes see,
but know that for all these things
God will bring you to judgment. *Ecclesiastes 11:9*

—SOLOMON, "THE PREACHER"

No sin is small.

—JEREMY TAYLOR

The lives we have led have left us such as we are today.

—JOHN B. DYKES

Do not take revenge, my friends, but leave room for God's wrath, for it is written: "It is mine to avenge; I will repay," says the Lord. *Romans 12:19*

—ST. PAUL

Free will enables us to choose; but it is grace that enables us to choose the good.

—BERNARD OF CLAIRVAUX

Seek the LORD while he may be found; call on him while he is near. *Isaiah 55:6*

—ISAIAH, THE PROPHET

Satan never slumbers, and we are admonished to "be vigilant."

—W.T. USSERY

Do everything without complaining or arguing,
so that you may become blameless and pure, children of God
without fault in a crooked and depraved generation,
in which you shine like stars in the universe. *Philippians 2:14-15*

—ST. PAUL

For prayer is nothing else than being on terms of
friendship with God.

—ST. TERESA OF AVILA

For the wisdom of this world is foolishness in God's sight.
1 Corinthians 3:19a

—ST. PAUL

Those who complain most are most to be complained of.

—MATTHEW HENRY

Unless men see a beauty and delight
in the worship of God, they will not do it willingly.

—JOHN OWEN

When you make a vow to God, do not delay in fulfilling it.
He has no pleasure in fools; fulfill your vow. It is better not to vow
than to make a vow and not fulfill it. *Ecclesiastes 5:4-5*

—SOLOMON, "THE PREACHER"

Guilt is the very nerve of sorrow.

—HORACE BUSHNELL

Throughout its nature and scope, Christianity exhibits proof of its Divine origin; and its practical precepts are no less pure than its doctrines are sublime.

—WILLIAM WILBERFORCE

Do not be overcome by evil, but overcome evil with good.

Romans 12:21

—ST. PAUL

Although we cannot intrude into the mysterious dealings of God, we can trust him to act with justice.

—J. VERNON MCGEE

A good name is better than fine perfume, and the day of death better than the day of birth. *Ecclesiastes 7:1*

—SOLOMON, "THE PREACHER"

Yielding to Christ is confessing every known sin in your life, yielding every area of your life. It means yielding your girlfriend, your boyfriend, your family, your business, your career, your ambitions, your soul, the innermost thoughts and depths of your heart; yielding them all to Christ, holding nothing back.

—BILLY GRAHAM

It is always easier to go with the crowd than to battle your way against it. It is always easier to conform than to be a nonconformist.

—WILLIAM BARCLAY

Flee from sexual immorality. All other sins a man commits are outside his body, but he who sins sexually sins against his own body. *1 Corinthians 6:18*

—ST. PAUL

Jesus has merited the title of the Great Physician not primarily
because of the specific illnesses which he cured,
but because he put the body in its proper place in the wholeness
of life. He did heal men's bodies, but he told them that if they
would seek first the Kingdom of God, their bodily needs would fall
into their proper and secondary place.

—RALPH W. SOCKMAN

Marriage was ordained by God,
instituted in paradise, was the relief of a natural necessity,
and the first blessing from the Lord.

—JEREMY TAYLOR

Be on your guard; stand firm in the faith; be men of courage;
be strong. Do everything in love. *1 Corinthians 16:13-14*

—ST. PAUL

There is nothing better than peace,
by which all strife in heaven and earth is done away.
—IGNATIUS OF ANTIOCH

Let us be out and out
for Christ; let us give no uncertain sound.
—DWIGHT L. MOODY

Cast your bread upon the waters, for after many days
you will find it again. *Ecclesiastes 11:1*
—SOLOMON, "THE PREACHER"

A tree has to be planted
before it can spread its branches.
—THEODORE PARKER FERRIS

If we live, we live to the Lord;
and if we die, we die to the Lord. So, whether we live or die,
we belong to the Lord. *Romans 14:8*

—ST. PAUL

God never placed a Christian in a condition that he could not
see something to do, if he would but look.

—W.T. USSERY

I will save you from the hands
of the wicked and redeem you from the grasp of the cruel.

Jeremiah 15:21

—JEREMIAH, THE PROPHET

Holy and without blame we are not; holy and without blame
God may intend us to be, although we cannot or will not believe it;
but holy and without blame before him we yearn to be with
unquenchable longing—and we are never at peace until in some
measure this shall become true for us, of us, in us.

—JOHN L. CASTEEL

Expect great things from God; attempt great things for God.

—WILLIAM CAREY

And we know that in all things
God works for the good of those who love him, who have been
called according to his purpose. *Romans 8:28*

—ST. PAUL

Every condition of life has its perils and its advantages;
and the office of religion is, not to change that in which Providence
has placed us, but to strengthen and sanctify our hearts that
we may resist the temptations, and improve the opportunities of
blessings presented to us.

—GEORGE WASHINGTON BETHUNE

Therefore, my dear brothers, stand firm.
Let nothing move you. Always give yourselves fully to the work of
the Lord, because you know that
your labor in the Lord is not in vain. *1 Corinthians 15:58*

—ST. PAUL

Trust God for great things; with your five loaves and two fishes,
He will show you a way to feed thousands.

—HORACE BUSHNELL

Since no man knows the future,
who can tell him what is to come? *Ecclesiastes 8:7*

—SOLOMON, "THE PREACHER"

Carry the cross patiently, and with perfect submission;
and in the end it shall carry you.

—THOMAS À KEMPIS

Do not allow the excitement of entering into
devotional literature detract you from the priority you give to
Bible study and meditation on the Scriptures.

—BERNARD OF CLAIRVAUX

I consider that our present sufferings are not worth comparing
with the glory that will be revealed in us. *Romans 8:18*

—ST. PAUL

Sow an act, and you reap a habit; sow a habit, and you reap a character; sow a character, and you reap a destiny.

—GEORGE DANA BOARDMAN

The Gospel offers something to us, but it also demands something from us.

—ROLLAND W. SCHLOERB

Do not be misled: "Bad company corrupts good character."
1 Corinthians 15:33

—ST. PAUL

The Lord only requires two things of us: that we should love God and love our neighbor.

—ST. TERESA OF AVILA

If I speak in the tongues of men and of angels,
but have not love, I am only
a resounding gong or a clanging cymbal. *1 Corinthians 13:1*

—ST. PAUL

Unbelievers do not have a love of God's truth in their
heart *2 Thessalonians 2:10.* As a result, they have erroneous beliefs
about God and, because it is based on those beliefs,
a wrong value system. Their wrong concept of God results in an
idolatrous value system.

—DON CROSSLAND

It should be the lesson of our life to
grow into a holy independence of every judgment which has not
the sanction of conscience and of God.

—JAMES W. ALEXANDER

Do not revile the king even in your thoughts,
or curse the rich in your bedroom, because a bird of the air may
carry your words, and a bird on the wing may
report what you say. *Ecclesiastes 10:20*

—SOLOMON, "THE PREACHER"

Every step toward Christ kills a doubt. Every thought,
word, and deed for Him carries you away from discouragement.

—THEODORE L. CUYLER

For God is not a God of disorder but of peace.
1 Corinthians 14:33a

—ST. PAUL

To receive Christ's help, we must wait upon him.

—JOHN OWEN

$\mathbb{B}$ut true Christians consider themselves as not satisfying some rigorous creditor, but as discharging a debt of gratitude.

—WILLIAM WILBERFORCE

$\mathbb{F}$or the wages of sin is death, but the gift of God is eternal life in Christ Jesus our Lord. *Romans 6:23*

—ST. PAUL

$\mathbb{W}$e must know our Bible so truly that when we do not have it between covers we still have it.

—HAMPTON ADAMS

$\mathbb{A}$ mighty fortress is our God, a bulwark never failing; our helper He, amid the flood of mortal ills prevailing.

—MARTIN LUTHER

And now these three remain: faith, hope and love. But the
greatest of these is love. *1 Corinthians 13:13*

—ST. PAUL

Despite the weakness and triviality of
many modern churches, it is an organism, a living fellowship;
the body of Christ animated by his spirit,
directed by his mind, acting as an instrument of his loving
and redeeming purpose.

—DAVID A. MACLENNAN

How beautiful on the mountains are the feet of those who
bring good news, who proclaim peace,
who bring good tidings, who proclaim salvation, who say to Zion,
"Your God reigns!" *Isaiah 52:7*

—ISAIAH, THE PROPHET

89

The early Christian was not called from a social unity into "splendid isolation"; he was called into "a household of faith."

—HAROLD A. BOSLEY

The believer is to use his liberty, not abuse it.

—J. VERNON MCGEE

When times are good, be happy; but when times are bad, consider: God has made the one
as well as the other. Therefore, a man cannot discover anything about his future. *Ecclesiastes 7:14*

—SOLOMON, "THE PREACHER"

There is no salvation outside the church.

—CYPRIAN

Therefore let us stop passing judgment on one another. Instead, make up your mind not to put any stumbling block or obstacle in your brother's way. *Romans 14:13*

—ST. PAUL

Thy way, not mine, O Lord, however dark it be; lead me by thine own hand; choose out the path for me.

—HORATIUS BONAR

"There is no peace," says the LORD, "for the wicked." *Isaiah 48:22*

—ISAIAH, THE PROPHET

Outside the church is no truth, no Christ, no blessedness.

—MARTIN LUTHER

Too many persons seem to use their religion as a diver does his
bell, to venture down into the depths of worldliness
with safety, and there grope for pearls, with just so much of
heaven's air as will keep them from suffocating,
and no more; and some, alas! as at times is the case with the diver,
are suffocated in the experiment.

—GEORGE B. CHEEVER

For God, who said, "Let light shine out of darkness,"
made his light shine in our hearts to give us the light of the
knowledge of the glory of God
in the face of Christ. *2 Corinthians 4:6*

—ST. PAUL

It is better to keep quiet and be real,
than to chatter and be unreal. It is a good thing to teach if, that is,
the teacher practices what he preaches.

—IGNATIUS OF ANTIOCH

When the ungodly see that Christian people do not repent,
you cannot expect them to repent and turn away from their sins.

—DWIGHT L. MOODY

As dead flies give perfume a bad smell, so a little folly
outweighs wisdom and honor. *Ecclesiastes 10:1*

—SOLOMON, "THE PREACHER"

All my theology is reduced to this narrow compass,
"Jesus Christ came into the world to save sinners."

—ARCHIBALD ALEXANDER

Love does not delight in evil but rejoices with the truth.
1 Corinthians 13:6

—ST. PAUL

I heard a man on television say that only one
New Testament Scripture speaks of restoration. My question for
him is "How many references does it take?"

—DON CROSSLAND

Therefore do not let sin reign in your mortal body so that
you obey its evil desires. *Romans 6:12*

—ST. PAUL

Every generation needs to rethink, restate,
and creatively apply its theological heritage to its own situation.
In this way the heritage stays vital, and relevant.

—MILDRED BANGS WYNKOOP

Let us, then, attach ourselves to those who are religiously
devoted to peace, and not to those who are for it hypocritically.

—CLEMENT OF ROME

For the foolishness of God is wiser than
man's wisdom, and the weakness of God is stronger than
man's strength. *1 Corinthians 1:25*

—ST. PAUL

No man can have God as his Father who has not the church as his Mother.

—JOHN CALVIN

Although a wicked man commits a hundred crimes and still lives a long time, I know that it will go better with God-fearing men, who are reverent before God. Yet because the wicked do not fear God, it will not go well with them, and their days will not lengthen like a shadow. *Ecclesiastes 8:12-13*

—SOLOMON, "THE PREACHER"

There is no such thing as a solitary Christian.

—JOHN WESLEY

The injuries of life, if rightly improved,
will be to us as the strokes of the statuary on his marble,
forming us to a more beautiful shape,
and making us fitter to adorn the heavenly temple.

—COTTON MATHER

This is what the LORD says:
"Cursed is the one who trusts in man, who depends on flesh
for his strength and whose heart
turns away from the LORD." *Jeremiah 17:5*

—JEREMIAH, THE PROPHET

The church is of God, called by God, gathered by
God for divine purposes. This constitutes the value of the church,
its importance, and its permanence.

—R. BROKHOFF

Prayer is the wing wherewith the soul flies to heaven,
and meditation the eye wherewith we see God.

—AMBROSE OF MILAN

For our light and momentary troubles are achieving for us an
eternal glory that far outweighs them all. *2 Corinthians 4:17*

—ST. PAUL

Habits are to the soul what the veins and
arteries are to the blood, the courses in which it moves.

—HORACE BUSHNELL

For too many the designation Protestant means something
negative. It can easily signify that one is against
something. But originally to be a Protestant was to be
a witness of a great faith and conviction. It derives
from the primary meaning of the word *protestari* which means
to make an affirmation, to express a conviction,
to make an avowal of a faith, to witness to a great reality of truth.

—CLIFFORD ANSGAR NELSON

If the ax is dull and its edge unsharpened, more
strength is needed but skill will bring success. *Ecclesiastes 10:10*

—SOLOMON, "THE PREACHER"

You can always tell when a man is a great way from God—when
he is always talking about himself and how good he is.

—DWIGHT L. MOODY

If there be ground for you to trust in your own righteousness, then, all that Christ did to purchase salvation, and all that God did to prepare the way for it is in vain.

—JONATHAN EDWARDS

So we fix our eyes not on what is seen, but on what is unseen. For what is seen is temporary, but what is unseen is eternal. *2 Corinthians 4:18*

—ST. PAUL

Science is beginning to catch up with Jesus in his understanding of the role of faith, hope, and love in the cure of disease and the maintenance of health.

—ALBERT EDWARD DAY

We do not always come through our testings as
we wish we would. Yet time after time we are brought back to our
tasks with renewed determination because of the trust
our Lord puts in us. And always we seem to feel the assurance that
through him the victory will be won.

—GERALD KENNEDY

Who is like the wise man? Who knows the
explanation of things? Wisdom brightens a man's face and
changes its hard appearance. *Ecclesiastes 8:1*

—SOLOMON, "THE PREACHER"

God reaches in two directions:
He reaches down and He reaches out.

—RALPH A. HERRING

 So do not fear, for I am with you; do not be dismayed, for I am your God. I will strengthen you and help you; I will uphold you with my righteous right hand. *Isaiah 41:10*

—ISAIAH, THE PROPHET

Does the phrase "in Christ" or "in union with Christ" puzzle you? To many people the words are meaningless, which of course indicates that the new life has never invaded them. Yet these people apparently know what you mean when you say that you are in politics, in law, in business, or in advertising.

—PAUL S. REES

If ever a man could have felt the church
to be unnecessary, he was Jesus. Yet he did not stay away from the
"church" of his day. It was his custom to go to the
synagogue on the Sabbath, and he made many trips to the temple.

—R. BROKHOFF

No man can lift up his head with manly calmness and peace
who is the slave of other men's judgments.

—JAMES W. ALEXANDER

We live by faith, not by sight.
We are confident, I say, and would prefer to be away from the
body and at home with the Lord. *2 Corinthians 5:7*

—ST. PAUL

But deep within ourselves, if we persevere
in patience and fidelity, we will again and again be given some
intimation of the work God is bringing to pass in us: the
restoration of the clean heart, the re-creation of the right spirit,
and the secret growth of his own divine beauty and righteousness
within us. And we shall be amazed at his grace, and
shall find ourselves possessed of joy which passes understanding.

—JOHN L. CASTEEL

Don't you know that you yourselves are God's temple and that
God's Spirit lives in you? *1 Corinthians 3:16*

—ST. PAUL

I have seen something else under the sun:
The race is not to the swift or the battle to the strong, nor does
food come to the wise or wealth to the brilliant or
favor to the learned; but time and chance happen to them all.

Ecclesiastes 9:11

—SOLOMON, "THE PREACHER"

Hating people is like burning down your own
house to get rid of a rat.

—HARRY EMERSON FOSDICK

We have not only to be called Christians, but to be Christians.

—IGNATIUS OF ANTIOCH

Therefore, if anyone is in Christ, he is a new creation; the old has gone, the new has come! *2 Corinthians 5:17*

—ST. PAUL

The best advertisement of a work-shop is first-class work.
The strongest attraction to
Christianity is a well-made Christian character.

—THEODORE L. CUYLER

Even youths grow tired and weary, and young men stumble and fall; but those who hope in the Lord will renew their strength. They will soar on wings like eagles; they will run and not grow weary, they will walk and not be faint. *Isaiah 40:30-31*

—ISAIAH, THE PROPHET

The remedy for the present threatened decay of faith is not a more stalwart creed or a more unflinching acceptance of it, but a profoundly spiritual life.

—LYMAN ABBOTT

Do not be quickly provoked in your spirit, for anger resides in the lap of fools. *Ecclesiastes 7:9*

—SOLOMON, "THE PREACHER"

The Great Commission was not given to the Christian ministry but to the Christian church.

—JOHN A. REDHEAD

Serve God in fear and in truth, forsaking empty talkativeness and the erroneous teaching of the crowd.

—POLYCARP OF SMYRNA

The grass withers and the flowers fall, but the word of our God stands forever. *Isaiah 40:8*

—ISAIAH, THE PROPHET

It is not too much to say that, second only to faith in God, our human relationships are the most important thing in our lives.

—SAMUEL M. SHOEMAKER

Three times I pleaded with the Lord to take it away from me. But he said to me, "My grace is sufficient for you, for my power is made perfect in weakness." Therefore I will boast all the more gladly about my weaknesses, so that Christ's power may rest on me. That is why, for Christ's sake, I delight in weaknesses, in insults, in hardships, in persecutions, in difficulties. For when I am weak, then I am strong. *2 Corinthians 12:8-10*

—ST. PAUL

As a man goes down in self, he goes up in God.
—GEORGE B. CHEEVER

A man's neighbor is everyone who needs help.
—CUNNINGHAM GEIKIE

Though I am free and belong to no man, I make myself a slave to everyone, to win as many as possible. *1 Corinthians 9:19*
—ST. PAUL

Regardless of the terms in which equality may be debated in other arenas, Christianity proposes to ignore the relative historical achievements and standards of people to raise everyone into the equality of fellowship as children of God.
—DUKE K. MCCALL

No man has power over the wind to contain it; so no one has power over the day of his death. As no one is discharged in time of war, so wickedness will not release those who practice it. *Ecclesiastes 8:8*

—SOLOMON, "THE PREACHER"

It is a shame for a man to desire honor only because of his noble progenitors, and not to deserve it by his own virtue.

—JOHN CHRYSOSTOM

But God demonstrates his own love for us in this: While we were still sinners, Christ died for us. *Romans 5:8*

—ST. PAUL

It was pride that changed angels into devils;
it is humility that makes men as angels.
—ST. AUGUSTINE

We have traveled the road to
Bethlehem so often that it is for us a familiar journey.
But we can never exhaust its meaning.
—HAROLD COOKE PHILLIPS

But the fruit of the Spirit is love,
joy, peace, patience, kindness, goodness, faithfulness,
gentleness and self-control.
Against such things there is no law. *Galatians 5:22-23*
—ST. PAUL

Easter is the story of a discovery, the discovery
that Christ lives. He is alive in the world.
It has taken one deep fear out of life, the fear of death.
—JOSEPH R. SIZOO

The heart of the wise is in the house of mourning,
but the heart of fools is in the house of pleasure. *Ecclesiastes 7:4*
—SOLOMON, "THE PREACHER"

They crucified Jesus not
because they disliked what he said, but because
they couldn't take it!
—PAUL SHERER

But blessed is the man who trusts in the LORD,
whose confidence is in him.
He will be like a tree planted by the water that
sends out its roots by the stream.
It does not fear when heat comes; its leaves are always green.
It has no worries in a year of
drought and never fails to bear fruit. *Jeremiah 17:7-8*

—JEREMIAH, THE PROPHET

Rather than offend God,
let us offend foolish and stupid men who exalt themselves and
boast with their pretensions to fine speech.

—CLEMENT OF ROME

Numbers are essential,
but not absolutely essential to strength. For many churches are
numerically strong but lamentably weak spiritually.
Numbers, then, are no display of spiritual power or strength.

—W.T. USSERY

Let us not become conceited,
provoking and envying each other. *Galatians 5:26*

—ST. PAUL

Nothing sets a person so much out of
the devil's reach as humility.

—JONATHAN EDWARDS

The Jesus that men want
to see is not the Jesus they really need to see.
—G. CAMPBELL MORGAN

For there is a proper time and procedure
for every matter, though a man's misery weighs heavily
upon him. *Ecclesiastes 8:6*
—SOLOMON, "THE PREACHER"

Let none of you hold anything against his neighbor.
Do not give the heathen opportunities whereby God's people
should be scoffed at through the stupidity of a few.
For, "Woe to him by whose folly my name is scoffed at before any."
—IGNATIUS OF ANTIOCH

A tender conscience is an inestimable blessing;
that is, a conscience not only quick
to discern what is evil, but instantly to shun it, as the eyelid
closes itself against the mote.

—NEHEMIAH ADAMS

Carry each other's burdens, and in this way you will
fulfill the law of Christ. *Galatians 6:2*

—ST. PAUL

God is the God of truth;
and every spiritual quality must live with that holy attribute.

—EDWIN HOLT HUGHES

Words from a wise man's mouth are gracious,
but a fool is consumed by his own lips. *Ecclesiastes 10:12*

—SOLOMON, "THE PREACHER"

Every valley shall be raised up, every mountain and hill made
low; the rough ground shall become level,
the rugged places a plain. And the glory of the LORD will be
revealed, and all mankind together will see it.
For the mouth of the LORD has spoken. *Isaiah 40:4, 5*

—ISAIAH, THE PROPHET

Every man's life is a plan of God.

—HORACE BUSHNELL

He that lives to live forever, never fears dying.
—WILLIAM PENN

Each one should test his own actions.
Then he can take pride in himself, without comparing himself to
somebody else, for each one
should carry his own load. *Galatians 6:4-5*
—ST. PAUL

No disciple who aspires to a vigorous spiritual life
can afford to neglect the Bible.
—CLOVIS G. CHAPPELL

The greatest thing of all in giving pleasure to God is love.
It is impossible to please Him unless
there be some knowledge of His love in our hearts and
some love to Him in return.

—G.B.F. HALLOCK

Love is patient, love is kind.
It does not envy, it does not boast, it is not proud.

1 Corinthians 13:4

—ST. PAUL

The true recipe for a miserable existence is
to quarrel with Providence.

—JAMES W. ALEXANDER

Wisdom makes one wise man more powerful than ten rulers in a city. *Ecclesiastes 7:19*

—SOLOMON, "THE PREACHER"

It is better to remember life than death. And best of all is it to live with Christ every day. That is the best preparation for immortal life.

—JAMES LEARMOUNT

If I give all I possess to the poor and surrender my body to the flames, but have not love, I gain nothing. *1 Corinthians 13:3*

—ST. PAUL

The tortue of a bad conscience is the hell of a living soul.

—JOHN CALVIN

A little while ago a Sunday school teacher in the last stage of rapid consumption was asked by a friend who visited her, "Are you afraid to die?" "I am not going to die," was her cheerful reply as she pointed to the motto that hung upon the wall of her chamber which read, "The gift of God is eternal life." She believed that those words were true, and so she knew and was confident that for her there was no death. It is Jesus who died. And because He has died and risen again we need never die.

—ALFRED BARRATT

Do not be deceived: God cannot be mocked. A man reaps what he sows. *Galatians 6:7*

—ST. PAUL

The shifting systems of false religion are continually changing their places; but the gospel of Christ is the same forever. While other false lights are extinguished, this true light ever shineth.

—THEODORE L. CUYLER

Wisdom is better than weapons of war, but one sinner destroys much good. *Ecclesiastes 9:18*

—SOLOMON, "THE PREACHER"

Big purposes free us from petty fretfulness and little ailments.

—RALPH W. SOCKMAN

The great fundamental principle of the Reformation was the individual responsibility of the human soul to its Maker and Judge.

—TALBOT WILSON CHAMBERS

My people will live in peaceful dwelling places,
in secure homes, in undisturbed places of rest. *Isaiah 32:18*

—ISAIAH, THE PROPHET

One of the self-authenticating truths which we come at last
to acknowledge is this strange fact: that we know
that for the evil in our lives we ourselves are responsible, but for
the good God alone deserves the praise.

—JOHN L. CASTEEL

If our religion only proclaims
a high standard of ethics, then our religion is a burden heavier
than we can bear.

—ROLLAND W. SCHLOERB

Let us not become weary in doing good, for at the proper time we will reap a harvest if we do not give up. *Galatians 6:9*

—ST. PAUL

Refusal to join the church on the claim that a person can be a Christian outside the church is the confession of a grave sin. This refusal usually results from a sense of self-sufficiency, independence, and exclusiveness. These are manifestations of man's worst sin, pride.

—R. BROKHOFF

Wisdom is a shelter as money is a shelter, but the advantage of knowledge is this: that wisdom preserves the life of its possessor. *Ecclesiastes 7:12*

—SOLOMON, "THE PREACHER"

No man can quench his thirst with sand,
or with water from the Dead Sea; so no man can find rest
from his own character,
however good, or from his own acts, however religious.

—HORATIUS BONAR

I the LORD search the heart and examine the mind,
to reward a man according to his conduct, according to what
his deeds deserve. *Jeremiah 17:10*

—JEREMIAH, THE PROPHET

Grant that I may not pray alone with
the mouth; help me that I may pray from the depths of my heart.

—MARTIN LUTHER

Grant me no more than to be a sacrifice for God.

—IGNATIUS OF ANTIOCH

For we are God's workmanship,
created in Christ Jesus to do good works, which God prepared in
advance for us to do. *Ephesians 2:10*

—ST. PAUL

For a church to be our church, we must have
worshiped there, seen Christ lifted up, felt his presence, seen on
his face the light of the glory of God.
There in that presence we must have confessed our sins and
experienced the grace of forgiveness.

—HAMPTON ADAMS

No one can comprehend what goes on
under the sun. Despite all his efforts to search it out, man cannot
discover its meaning. Even if a wise man claims
he knows, he cannot really comprehend it. *Ecclesiastes 8:17*

—SOLOMON, "THE PREACHER"

Grace is but glory begun, and glory is but grace perfected.

—JONATHAN EDWARDS

The church is integral to the gospel.
Membership in the church is the expression in terms of this life of
the new relationship which men enjoy with
God and each other through what Christ has done for them.

—DAVID A. MACLENNAN

The fruit of righteousness will be peace; the effect of righteousness will be quietness and confidence forever. *Isaiah 32:17*

—ISAIAH, THE PROPHET

True repentance is to cease from sinning.

—AMBROSE OF MILAN

All the sin that has darkened human life and saddened human history began in believing a falsehood: all the power of Christianity to make men holy is associated with believing truth.

—JOHN ALBERT BROADUS

In him and through faith in him we may approach God with freedom and confidence. *Ephesians 3:12*

—ST. PAUL

There is no excuse for him who spontaneously abandons the external communion of a church in which the Word of God is preached and the sacraments are administered.

—JOHN CALVIN

Do not say, "Why were the old days better than these?" For it is not wise to ask such questions. *Ecclesiastes 7:10*

—SOLOMON, "THE PREACHER"

How blessed and amazing are God's gifts, dear friends! Life with immortality, splendor with righteousness, truth with confidence, faith with assurance, self-control with holiness! And all these things are within our comprehension.

—CLEMENT OF ROME

Yet the LORD longs to be gracious to you;

he rises to show you compassion. For the LORD is a God of justice.

Blessed are all who wait for him! *Isaiah 30:18*

—ISAIAH, THE PROPHET

The Lord gets His best soldiers out of the highlands of affliction.

—CHARLES HADDON SPURGEON

"In your anger do not sin":

Do not let the sun go down while you are still angry, and do not

give the devil a foothold. *Ephesians 4:26-27*

—ST. PAUL

The heart that is to be filled to the brim

with holy joy must be held still.

—GEORGE SEATON BOWES

Is the church essential to salvation? It is a necessary means of grace. A man is saved by faith in Christ. This faith is a gift of the Holy Spirit who is received through the word of God, the textbook of the church, and the sacraments which are necessary for that faith which saves the soul. The church then is the mother of our faith. As a mother is necessary for the birth of a child, the church is necessary for salvation.

—R. BROKHOFF

If a ruler's anger rises against you, do not leave your post; calmness can lay great errors to rest. *Ecclesiastes 10:4*

—SOLOMON, "THE PREACHER"

The narrow sectariansim of a church that wants to teach its
people that they are the only true church of Christ,
the domineering exclusiveness that refuses to acknowledge other
Christians as being members of a true and valid fellowship
of believers in Jesus Christ—that I regret. When the ministry of all
other churches is counted as not having a valid minstry,
and the sacraments of all other churches as not being proper and
valid in their efficacy before God, then I protest.

—CLIFFORD ANSGAR NELSON

Live as with God; and whatever be your calling, pray for
the gift that will perfectly qualify you in it.

—HORACE BUSHNELL

But the LORD is with me like a mighty warrior;
so my persecutors will stumble and not prevail. They will fail
and be thoroughly disgraced;
their dishonor will never be forgotten. *Jeremiah 20:11*

—JEREMIAH, THE PROPHET

Christian evangelism is not a call to occupy the rocking chair
of grace for the rest of one's natural—or unnatural—life.
It is a challenge to take to the road in the discipleship of Him who
will be forever on the road until the last man and the last
area of human life are redeemed.

—ALBERT EDWARD DAY

It is a truism that if you permit others to do the things
that in reality are yours to do, you will soon be obliged to do as
these others say you must do. Difficulty develops.
Work makes one strong. Laziness, shirking makes one weak.
We learn to bear responsibility
by bearing responsibility. There are benefits in service.

—G.B.F. HALLOCK

He who has been stealing must steal no longer, but must work,
doing something useful with his own hands, that he
may have something to share with those in need. *Ephesians 4:28*

—ST. PAUL

A church in prevailing prayer is a church in prevailing power.

—W.T. USSERY

It is better to go to a house of mourning than to go to a house of feasting, for death is the destiny of every man; the living should take this to heart. *Ecclesiastes 7:2*

—SOLOMON, "THE PREACHER"

Repentance, to be of any avail, must work a change of heart and conduct.

—THEODORE L. CUYLER

The ruthless will vanish, the mockers will disappear, and all who have an eye for evil will be cut down. *Isaiah 29:20*

—ISAIAH, THE PROPHET

All that Jesus does for us reflects only a small part of his concern in comparison with that which he desires to do through us.

—RALPH A. HERRING

The holiest of men still need Christ as their King, for God does not give them a stock of holiness. But unless they receive a supply each moment, nothing but unholiness would remain. Even perfect holiness is acceptable to God only through Jesus Christ.

—JOHN WESLEY

No temptation has seized you except what is common to man. And God is faithful; he will not let you be tempted beyond what you can bear. But when you are tempted, he will also provide a way out so that you can stand up under it. *1 Corinthians 10:13*

—ST. PAUL

The higher a man is in grace,
the lower he will be in his own esteem.
—CHARLES H. SPURGEON

Whoever digs a pit may fall into it; whoever
breaks through a wall may be bitten by a snake. *Ecclesiastes 10:8*
—SOLOMON, "THE PREACHER"

Humility, a blessed grace, smooths the furrows of care,
and gilds the dark paths of life. It will make us kind,
tender-hearted, affable, and enable us to do more for God and the
Gospel than the most fervent zeal without it.
—HENRY MARTYN

Do not let any unwholesome talk come out of your mouths, but only what is helpful for building others up according to their needs, that it may benefit those who listen. *Ephesians 4:29*

—ST. PAUL

The pastor is not a religious lecturer but a spiritual general who marshals the forces under his charge and trains them for their appointed service, for the recruiting of others for the building up of the body of Christ.

—JOHN A. REDHEAD

Nothing you can see has real value. Our God Jesus Christ, indeed, has revealed himself more clearly by returning to the Father.

—IGNATIUS OF ANTIOCH

Lord, you establish peace for us;
all that we have accomplished you have done for us. *Isaiah 26:12*

—ISAIAH, THE PROPHET

Resignation and faith behold God in the smallest
hair that falls; and the happiest life is that of him who has bound
together all the affairs of life,
great and small, and entrusted them to God.

—JAMES W. ALEXANDER

The Holy Spirit is a centrifugal force that
attracts believers into churches. The power of the Spirit is a divine
magnet which draws all men to Christ and to each other.

—R. BROKHOFF

The more the words, the less the meaning,
and how does that profit anyone? *Ecclesiastes 6:11*

—SOLOMON, "THE PREACHER"

Family education and order are some of the
chief means of grace; if these are duly maintained, all the means of
grace are likely to prosper and become effectual.

—JONATHAN EDWARDS

"Can anyone hide in secret places so that I
cannot see him?" declares the LORD. "Do not I fill heaven and earth?"
declares the LORD. *Jeremiah 23:24*

—JEREMIAH, THE PROPHET

$\mathbb{F}$ew people are ever "successful" as the world sees success
unless they know how to get along with other people;
and many fail, in the worldly sense and in the Christian sense also,
because they do not.

—SAMUEL M. SHOEMAKER

$\mathbb{M}$en who seek God do not poke and putter in the muck and
mire of the world; they lift their eyes unto the heavens.

—DUKE K. MCCALL

$\mathbb{S}$o whether you eat or drink or
whatever you do, do it all for the glory of God. *1 Corinthians 10:31*

—ST. PAUL

Christ is not a memory,
but a presence; not a figure in time, but a timeless figure.
—JOSEPH R. SIZOO

The quiet words of the wise are more to be heeded than the
shouts of a ruler of fools. *Ecclesiastes 9:17*
—SOLOMON, "THE PREACHER"

Christ gives us patience and fortitude to endure the things that
cannot be changed. But he also came to give us
courage to challenge the things which should be changed—
and wisdom to know the difference.
—RALPH W. SOCKMAN

The path of the righteous is level;
O upright One, you make the way of the righteous smooth. *Isaiah 26:7*

—ISAIAH, THE PROPHET

Stop thinking about your difficulties, whatever they are, and
start thinking about God instead.

—EMMET FOX

To those whom He counts worthy,
Christ gives the gift of suffering—not as a strange thing but as a
badge of honor, that we wear proudly in His name.

—BERNARD IDDINGS BELL

Be kind and compassionate to one another, forgiving
each other, just as in Christ God forgave you. *Ephesians 4:32*

—ST. PAUL

The primary task of the Church is not to mend the manners of the community, but to proclaim the matchless Gospel of the Lord Jesus Christ. When men hear that Gospel and believe it, their lives will give evidence of their faith.

—WALTER DALE LANGTRY

You will keep in perfect peace him whose mind is steadfast, because he trusts in you. Trust in the LORD forever, for the LORD, the LORD, is the Rock eternal. *Isaiah 26:3-4*

—ISAIAH, THE PROPHET

Do not talk Jesus Christ and set your heart on the world.

—IGNATIUS OF ANTIOCH

Naked a man comes from his mother's womb,
and as he comes, so he departs. He takes nothing from his labor
that he can carry in his hand. *Ecclesiastes 5:15*

—SOLOMON, "THE PREACHER"

Life was not planned to be a perpetual picnic for children
but a school for adult education.

—HERBERT WELCH

I have loved you with an everlasting love;
I have drawn you with loving-kindness. *Jeremiah 31:3b*

—JEREMIAH, THE PROPHET

When James writes in his epistle,
"purify your hearts" (4:8), the Greek wording shows a passive verb
which indicates that the purifying is done to us.
We can't purify our own hearts. God has to do this, but we can put
ourselves in the position to be purified by God.

—DON CROSSLAND

We must prostrate ourselves before the Master, and beseech
him with tears to have mercy on us and be reconciled to us and
bring us back to our honorable and holy practice of brotherly love.

—CLEMENT OF ROME

O Lord, you are my God; I will exalt you
and praise your name, for in perfect faithfulness you have done
marvelous things, things planned long ago. *Isaiah 25:1*

—ISAIAH, THE PROPHET

Do not pay attention to every word people say, or you may hear your servant cursing you—for you know in your heart that many times you yourself have cursed others. *Ecclesiastes 7:21-22*

—SOLOMON, "THE PREACHER"

Virtue consists in doing our duty in the various relations we sustain to ourselves, to our fellow-men, and to God, as it is made known by reason, revelation, and Providence.

—ARCHIBALD ALEXANDER

With joy you will draw water from the wells of salvation. *Isaiah 12:3*

—ISAIAH, THE PROPHET

On this side of the grave we are exiles, on that, citizens; on this side, orphans, on that, children; on this side, captives, on that, freemen; on this side disguised, unknown, on that, disclosed and proclaimed as the sons of God.

—HENRY WARD BEECHER

Be imitators of God, therefore, as dearly loved children and live a life of love, just as Christ loved us and gave himself up for us as a fragrant offering and sacrifice to God. *Ephesians 5:1-2*

—ST. PAUL

The best and noblest lives are those which are set toward high ideals. And the highest and noblest ideal that any man can have is Jesus of Nazareth.

—RENÈ ALMERON

We are all in the hands of an omnipotent, omniscient, just and merciful God, and whatever may be the destiny of humanity (for weal or woe), there will be a universal and eternal amen to all that God does.

—W.T. USSERY

Let us acknowledge the Lord; let us press on to acknowledge him. As surely as the sun rises, he will appear; he will come to us like the winter rains, like the spring rains that water the earth. *Hosea 6:3*

—HOSEA, THE PROPHET

Christ is not valued at all unless He is valued above all.
—ST. AUGUSTINE

Guard your steps when you go to the house of God.
Go near to listen rather than to offer the sacrifice of fools, who do
not know that they do wrong. *Ecclesiastes 5:1*
—SOLOMON, "THE PREACHER"

Knowledge is vain and
fruitless which is not reduced to practice.
—MATTHEW HENRY

It is one of the anomalies of our day that, while civilization
trembles at the possibility of destruction, the American people
spend more time than ever laughing themselves to death.
While hospitals are crowded with nervous and mental wrecks;
while suicide, crime, broken homes, and delinquency set
records, television clowns are paid fortunes to amuse us night
after night, turning tragedy into comedy. Never in history
has there been more ribald hilarity with less to be funny about.
Unfortunately, this attitude has spilled over into the church.

—VANCE HAVNER

Be very careful, then, how you live—
not as unwise but as wise, making the most of every opportunity,
because the days are evil. *Ephesians 5:15-16*

—ST. PAUL

A house is made to be lived in and not to be lived for.

—RALPH W. SOCKMAN

Surely God is my salvation;

I will trust and not be afraid. The LORD, the LORD, is my strength
and my song; he has become my salvation. *Isaiah 12:2*

—ISAIAH, THE PROPHET

In the midst of our ordinary affairs God breaks in upon us
and we learn, sooner or later, that the most inexorable fact of our
life is simply that he is never going to leave us alone.

—JOHN L. CASTEEL

The end of a matter is better than its beginning, and
patience is better than pride. *Ecclesiastes 7:8*

—SOLOMON, "THE PREACHER"

God hath promised pardon to him that repenteth,
but he hath not promised repentance to him that sinneth.

—ANSELM OF LAON

Resolve to live as with all your might while you do live, and as
you shall wish you had done ten thousand years hence.

—JONATHAN EDWARDS

For to us a child is born, to us a son is given, and the government
will be on his shoulders. And he will be called Wonderful
Counselor, Mighty God, Everlasting Father, Prince of Peace. *Isaiah 9:6*

—ISAIAH, THE PROPHET

If honor be your clothing, the suit will last a lifetime;
but if clothing be your honor, it will soon be worn threadbare.

—WILLIAM D. ARNOT

I am faithful to the duties of the present,
God will provide for the future.
—GREGORY T. BEDELL

Speak to one another with psalms, hymns and spiritual songs.
Sing and make music in your heart to the Lord,
always giving thanks to God the Father for everything, in the name
of our Lord Jesus Christ. *Ephesians 5:19-20*
—ST. PAUL

None but a theology that came out of
eternity can carry you and me safely to and through eternity.
—THEODORE L. CUYLER

And I saw that all labor and all achievement spring
from man's envy of his neighbor.
This too is meaningless, a chasing after the wind. *Ecclesiastes 4:4*

—SOLOMON, "THE PREACHER"

When men tell you to consult mediums and spiritists,
who whisper and mutter, should not a people inquire of their God?
Why consult the dead on behalf of the living? *Isaiah 8:19*

—ISAIAH, THE PROPHET

To endure the cross is not tragedy;
it is the suffering which is the fruit of an exclusive allegiance
to Jesus Christ.

—DIETRICH BONHOEFFER

Temptation always looks desirable to the one tempted.
Otherwise it would not be a temptation. But sin does not turn out
as good as it looks. It turns out very bad.

—G.B.F. HALLOCK

And pray in the Spirit on all occasions with
all kinds of prayers and requests. With this in mind, be alert and
always keep on praying for all the saints. *Ephesians 6:18*

—ST. PAUL

When an affluent society would coax us to believe that
happiness consists in the size of our automobiles, the
impressiveness of our houses, and the expensiveness of our
clothes, Jesus reminds us, "A man's life consisteth
not in the abundance of the things which he possesseth."

—MARTIN LUTHER KING

Prayer opens the heart to God, and it is the means by which the soul, though empty, is filled by God.

—JOHN BUNYAN

And afterward, I will pour out my Spirit on all people. Your sons and daughters will prophesy, your old men will dream dreams, your young men will see visions. *Joel 2:28*

—JOEL, THE PROPHET

The world is dying for want, not of good preaching, but of good hearing.

—GEORGE DANA BOARDMAN

It is better to heed a wise man's rebuke than to listen to the song of fools. *Ecclesiastes 7:5*

—SOLOMON, "THE PREACHER"

All unbelief is the belief of a lie.

—HORATIUS BONAR

If you do not stand firm in your faith, you will not stand at all.

Isaiah 7:9b

—ISAIAH, THE PROPHET

Every dollar dedicated to God and
His cause glorifies Him and strengthens His Kingdom.

—W.T. USSERY

The world is saying to the Church today:
We are sick and tired of listening to your debates and quarrels,
and your ecclesiastical contentions. We would see Jesus.

—G. CAMPBELL MORGAN

ut on the full armor of God so that you can take your stand against the devil's schemes. *Ephesians 6:11*

—ST. PAUL

It is well for the preacher to be mighty in organization, mighty in financiering, but it is better still for him to be mighty in the Scriptures.

—CLOVIS G. CHAPPELL

Woe to those who are wise in their own eyes and clever in their own sight. *Isaiah 5:21*

—ISAIAH, THE PROPHET

The New Testament makes it abundantly clear that whenever the Kingdom of God was concerned Jesus was absolutely uncompromising, even when he realized that for him personally the alternative to compromise was crucifixion.

—ERNEST FREMONT TITTLE

I thought in my heart, "God will bring to judgment both the righteous and the wicked, for there will be a time for every activity, a time for every deed." *Ecclesiastes 3:17*

—SOLOMON, "THE PREACHER"

Morality, taken as apart from religion, is but another name for decency in sin. It is just that negative species of virtue which consists in not doing what is scandalously depraved and wicked. But there is no heart of holy principle in it, any more than there is in the grosser sin.

—HORACE BUSHNELL

Faith comes by hearing the word of God. The church teaches and preaches the word of God. As men hear it with open minds and hearts, the Holy Spirit enters and creates this saving faith.

—R. BROKHOFF

Woe to the wicked! Disaster is upon them! They will be paid back for what their hands have done. *Isaiah 3:11*

—ISAIAH, THE PROPHET

Small deeds done are better than great deeds planned.
—PETER MARSHALL

Do we demonstrate before the world what we confess?
Is there anything about us and our movement that the world cannot
explain away, about which it must say God is at work?
—LEIGHTON FORD

Make it your ambition to lead a quiet life, to mind your own
business and to work with your hands, just as we told you,
so that your daily life may win the respect of outsiders and so that
you will not be dependent on anybody. *1 Thessalonians 4:11-12*
—ST. PAUL

Routine is God's way of
saving us between our times of inspiration.

—OSWALD CHAMBERS

Whatever we ask of God, let us also work toward it,
if there is anything we can do.

—JEREMY TAYLOR

From inside the fish Jonah prayed to the Lord his God. He said:
"In my distress I called to the Lord,
and he answered me. From the depths of the grave I called for
help, and you listened to my cry." *Jonah 2:1-2*

—JONAH, THE PROPHET

Plain horse sense ought to tell us that anything that makes no change in the man who professes it makes no difference to God, either.

—A.W. TOZER

Obedience means marching right on whether we feel it or not.

—D.L. MOODY

For God did not call us to be impure, but to live a holy life. *1 Thessalonians 4:7*

—ST. PAUL

I will set no value on anything I have or may possess except in relation to the Kingdom of God.

—DAVID LIVINGSTONE

Stop trusting in man, who has but a breath in his nostrils.
Of what account is he? *Isaiah 2:22*

—ISAIAH, THE PROPHET

The fewer the words, the better the prayer.

—MARTIN LUTHER

I denied myself nothing my eyes desired; I refused my heart no
pleasure. My heart took delight in all my work, and this
was the reward for all my labor. Yet when I surveyed all that my
hands had done and what I had toiled to achieve,
everything was meaningless, a chasing after the wind; nothing was
gained under the sun. *Ecclesiastes 2:10-11*

—SOLOMON, "THE PREACHER"

It is a little thing to trust God as far as we can see Him, so far as the way lies open before us; but to trust in Him when we are hedged in on every side and can see no way to escape, this is good and acceptable with God.

—JOHN WESLEY

Those who cling to worthless idols forfeit the grace that could be theirs. *Jonah 2:8*

—JONAH, THE PROPHET

The problem of unholy living does not stem from the fact that we desire to use money and time unwisely; the problem is that we do not intend to be as responsible and devout as we can.

—WILLIAM LAW

The affections of the godly are the same to everyone.
—BERNARD OF CLAIRVAUX

God never gave a man a thing to do,
concerning which it were irreverent to ponder how the
Son of God would have done it.
—GEORGE MACDONALD

Christ is the great central fact in the world's history;
to him everything looks forward or backward. All the lines of
history converge upon him. All march of providence is
guided by him. All the great purposes of God culminate in him.
The greatest and most momentous fact
which the history of the world records is the fact of his birth.
—CHARLES HADDON SPURGEON

Be joyful always; pray continually;
give thanks in all circumstances, for this is God's will for you in
Christ Jesus. *1 Thessalonians 5:16-18*

—ST. PAUL

It is in God's will that all true spirituality lies.

—ST. TERESA OF AVILA

The Christian life is not
merely knowing or hearing, but doing the will of Christ.

—FREDERICK W. ROBERTSON

The Lord your God is with you, he is mighty to save.
He will take great delight in you, he will quiet you with his love,
he will rejoice over you with singing. *Zephaniah 3:17*

—ZEPHANIAH, THE PROPHET

We need to attend diligently to the state of our soul, and to deal fervently and effectively with God about it.

—JOHN OWEN

There is no leveler like Christianity, but it levels by lifting all who receive it to the lofty table-land of a true character and of undying hope both for this world and the next.

—JONATHAN EDWARDS

This righteousness from God comes through faith in Jesus Christ to all who believe. There is no difference, for all have sinned and fall short of the glory of God, and are justified freely by his grace through the redemption that came by Christ Jesus. *Romans 3:22-24*

—ST. PAUL

Going to church doesn't make you a Christian any more than going to a garage makes you an automobile.

—WILLIAM A. ("BILLY") SUNDAY

God appoints our graces to be nurses to other men's weaknesses.

—HENRY WARD BEECHER

If I have the gift of prophecy and can fathom all mysteries and all knowledge, and if I have a faith that can move mountains, but have not love, I am nothing. *1 Corinthians 13:2*

—ST. PAUL

Whennow you and I will take the position that we're sinners and come to God and trust Christ as our Saviour—regardless of who we are, where we are, how we are or when we are—God will save us.

—J. VERNON MCGEE

"Come now, let us reason together," says the LORD. "Though your sins are like scarlet, they shall be as white as snow; though they are red as crimson, they shall be like wool." *Isaiah 1:18*

—ISAIAH, THE PROPHET

Scripture considers sin rebellion against the sovereignty of God.

—WILLIAM WILBERFORCE

The Christian ministry is the worst of all trades, but the best of all professions.

—JOHN NEWTON

Now all has been heard; here is the
conclusion of the matter: Fear God and keep his commandments,
for this is the whole duty of man. *Ecclesiastes 12:13*

—SOLOMON, "THE PREACHER"

There is no greater privilege in the world than serving
Christ and His Kingdom.

—JAMES L. MATHEWS